DNS and BIND on IPv6

DNS and BIND on IPv6

Cricket Liu

Beijing · Cambridge · Farnham · Köln · Sebastopol · Tokyo

DNS and BIND on IPv6

by Cricket Liu

Copyright © 2011 Cricket Liu. All rights reserved.
Printed in the United States of America.

Published by O'Reilly Media, Inc., 1005 Gravenstein Highway North, Sebastopol, CA 95472.

O'Reilly books may be purchased for educational, business, or sales promotional use. Online editions are also available for most titles (*http://my.safaribooksonline.com*). For more information, contact our corporate/institutional sales department: (800) 998-9938 or *corporate@oreilly.com*.

Editor: Mike Loukides
Production Editor: Holly Bauer
Proofreader: Holly Bauer

Cover Designer: Karen Montgomery
Interior Designer: David Futato
Illustrator: Robert Romano

Printing History:

    May 2011:   First Edition.

ISBN: 978-1-449-30519-2

[LSI]

1304703382

Table of Contents

Preface vii

1. **DNS and IPv6** 1
   Background   1
   IPv6 and DNS   2
   The ABCs of IPv6 Addresses   2
   IPv6 Forward and Reverse Mapping   4
   AAAA and ip6.arpa   5
   Adding AAAA Records to Forward-Mapping Zones   5
   IPv6 Reverse-Mapping Zones   6
   Delegation and Reverse-Mapping Zones   7
   Built-In Empty Reverse-Mapping Zones   8

2. **BIND on IPv6** 11
   Listening for Queries   11
   Sending Queries   12
   More on Query Port Randomization   12
   Forcing the Use of a Particular Protocol   13
   IPv6 Masters and Slaves   13
   Other IPv6 Zone Transfer Controls   14
   IPv6 Networks and Addresses in ACLs   15
   Registering IPv6 Name Servers   16
   Delegating to IPv6 Name Servers   16
   Server Statements for IPv6 Name Servers   17
   Special Considerations   17
       Handling "Monolingual" Name Servers   17
       Handling Broken Resolvers   18
   rndc and IPv6   19

3. **Resolver Configuration** 21
   Mac OS X   21

Windows		22
Dynamic Resolver Configuration		24
Resolver Configuration Using DHCPv6		25
Resolver Configuration Using Router Advertisements		25

4. DNS64 . . . . **27**

Authoritative Name Servers and DNS64	30
Interaction Between DNS64 and DNSSEC	30
DNS64 and Reverse Mapping	31

5. Troubleshooting **33**

nslookup	33
dig	35

Preface

I'm sorry for writing this ebook.

Well, that's not quite accurate. What I mean is, I'm sorry I didn't have time to update *DNS and BIND* to include all this new IPv6 material. *DNS and BIND* deserves a sixth edition, but I'm afraid my schedule is so hectic right now that I just don't have time to write it. Heck, I'm on a flight from Boston to Tampa as I write this. (Long flights are great for writing prefaces, not so great for writing books about Internet technologies. Though in-flight Internet access does help.)

This book is essentially all the material related to IPv6 that I would have included in the sixth edition of *DNS and BIND* (and *will*, once I get to it). It covers how DNS was extended to accommodate IPv6 addresses, both for forward-mapping and reverse-mapping. It describes how to configure a BIND name server to run on an IPv6 network and how to troubleshoot problems with IPv6 forward- and reverse-mapping. It even covers DNS64, a DNS-based transition technology that, together with a companion technology called NAT64, can help islands of IPv6-only speaking hosts communicate with IPv4 resources.

Audience

I wrote this book for DNS administrators who are rolling out IPv6 on their networks and who need to understand how to support IPv6 on those networks with DNS. This ebook covers the underlying theory, including the structure and representation of IPv6 addresses; the A, M, and O flags in Router Advertisements and what they mean to DNS; as well as the nuts and bolts, including the syntax of AAAA records and PTR records in the *ip6.arpa* reverse-mapping zone and the syntax and semantics of configuring a BIND name server.

Assumptions This Book Makes

This book assumes that you understand basic DNS theory and BIND configuration. It doesn't explain what a resource record is or how to edit a zone data file, or remind you that you need to increment the serial number of the zone's SOA record before reloading it (other than just now)—for that, I highly recommend *DNS and BIND*. But that shouldn't surprise you.

The book *doesn't* assume that you know anything in particular about IPv6, though.

Contents of This Book

This book is organized into five chapters as follows:

Chapter 1, *DNS and IPv6*

> This chapter explains the motivation behind the move to IPv6 and describes the structure and representation of IPv6 addresses. It also introduces the syntaxes of AAAA records and PTR records in the *ip6.arpa* IPv6 reverse-mapping zone and explains how to delegate subdomains of *ip6.arpa* zones.

Chapter 2, *BIND on IPv6*

> This chapter describes how to configure BIND name servers to run on IPv6 networks, including how to configure IPv6 master and slave name servers, how to use IPv6 addresses and networks in ACLs, and how to register and delegate to IPv6-speaking name servers. The chapter also includes a section on special considerations that may arise because IPv6 connectivity is not yet pervasive.

Chapter 3, *Resolver Configuration*

> This chapter shows how to configure popular stub resolvers (Linux/Unix, Mac OS X and Windows) to query IPv6-speaking name servers. It also covers dynamic configuration of resolvers using DHCPv6 and Router Advertisements.

Chapter 4, *DNS64*

> This chapter explains the DNS64 transition technology, which allows clients with IPv6-only network stacks to communicate with IPv4 servers.

Chapter 5, *Troubleshooting*

> This chapter describes how to use the common *nslookup* and *dig* troubleshooting tools to look up the IPv6 addresses of a domain name or reverse-map an IPv6 address to a domain name. It also covers how to query a name server's IPv6 address.

Conventions Used in This Book

The following typographical conventions are used in this book:

Plain text

> Indicates menu titles, menu options, menu buttons, and keyboard accelerators (such as Alt and Ctrl).

Italic

> Indicates new terms, URLs, email addresses, filenames, file extensions, pathnames, directories, and Unix utilities.

`Constant width`

    Indicates commands, options, switches, variables, attributes, keys, functions, types, classes, namespaces, methods, modules, properties, parameters, values, objects, events, event handlers, XML tags, HTML tags, macros, the contents of files, or the output from commands.

`Constant width bold`

    Shows commands or other text that should be typed literally by the user.

`Constant width italic`

    Shows text that should be replaced with user-supplied values.

 This icon signifies a tip, suggestion, or general note.

 This icon indicates a warning or caution.

Using Code Examples

This book is here to help you get your job done. In general, you may use the code in this book in your programs and documentation. You do not need to contact us for permission unless you're reproducing a significant portion of the code. For example, writing a program that uses several chunks of code from this book does not require permission. Selling or distributing a CD-ROM of examples from O'Reilly books does require permission. Answering a question by citing this book and quoting example code does not require permission. Incorporating a significant amount of example code from this book into your product's documentation does require permission.

We appreciate, but do not require, attribution. An attribution usually includes the title, author, publisher, and ISBN. For example: "*DNS and BIND on IPv6* by Cricket Liu (O'Reilly). Copyright 2011 Cricket Liu, 978-1-449-30519-2."

If you feel your use of code examples falls outside fair use or the permission given above, feel free to contact us at *permissions@oreilly.com*.

Safari® Books Online

 Safari Books Online is an on-demand digital library that lets you easily search over 7,500 technology and creative reference books and videos to find the answers you need quickly.

With a subscription, you can read any page and watch any video from our library online. Read books on your cell phone and mobile devices. Access new titles before they are available for print, and get exclusive access to manuscripts in development and post feedback for the authors. Copy and paste code samples, organize your favorites, download chapters, bookmark key sections, create notes, print out pages, and benefit from tons of other time-saving features.

O'Reilly Media has uploaded this book to the Safari Books Online service. To have full digital access to this book and others on similar topics from O'Reilly and other publishers, sign up for free at *http://my.safaribooksonline.com*.

How to Contact Us

Please address comments and questions concerning this book to the publisher:

O'Reilly Media, Inc.
1005 Gravenstein Highway North
Sebastopol, CA 95472
(800) 998-9938 (in the United States or Canada)
(707) 829-0515 (international or local)
(707) 829-0104 (fax)

We have a web page for this book, where we list errata, examples, and any additional information. You can access this page at:

http://www.oreilly.com/catalog/9781449305192

To comment or ask technical questions about this book, send email to:

bookquestions@oreilly.com

For more information about our books, courses, conferences, and news, see our website at *http://www.oreilly.com*.

Find us on Facebook: *http://facebook.com/oreilly*

Follow us on Twitter: *http://twitter.com/oreillymedia*

Watch us on YouTube: *http://www.youtube.com/oreillymedia*

Acknowledgments

Many thanks to my long-time editor, Mike Loukides, for suggesting this book in the first place. (Though now he's going to start pressuring me to get going on the sixth edition of *DNS and BIND*.) Thanks also to my boss at Infoblox, Steve Nye, who supported the project, and to my old friend and co-conspirator in the Ask Mr. DNS podcast, Matt Larson, who helps keep my DNS skills from atrophying completely. And much credit is due Owen DeLong for his excellent technical review.

Most of all, though, thanks to my family: Walt and Greta, Charlie and Jessie, and especially my wife, Paige. They give me both the time to write, and the reason.

CHAPTER 1

DNS and IPv6

Background

In early February 2011, the Internet Assigned Numbers Authority, or IANA, assigned the last remaining IPv4 address space to the five Regional Internet Registries (RIRs). As of this writing, the RIRs haven't yet doled out that address space to carriers and other customers, but it's clear that the exhaustion of IPv4 address space is imminent.

For most organizations on the Internet, the depletion of the Internet's unallocated IPv4 address space won't necessitate immediate changes—IPv4 isn't going anywhere for the foreseeable future. In certain exceptional cases, however, organizations may need to implement IPv6 almost right away: mobile carriers and ISPs seeking to expand their subscriber bases, for example, may need to use IPv6 for new subscribers if they lack additional IPv4 address space to use for expansion.

The Internet's transition from IPv4 to IPv6 has begun. With the US government's mandate that government agencies move their networks to IPv6, a growing number of users will access the Internet over the new protocol, and an increasing number of resources —websites, name servers, mail servers, and more—will be accessible via IPv6. In some cases, some may *only* be accessible over IPv6.

The transition to IPv6 will take years, maybe decades, to complete. Today, of course, IPv6 is already routed over the Internet: 9% of the Internet's Autonomous Systems advertise routes to both IPv4 and IPv6 networks. But IPv6 constitutes a tiny fraction of the traffic routed over the Internet. Organizations deploying new IPv6 networks today need to implement transition technologies that enable their IPv6-based devices to reach IPv4-only services.

Over time, however, the balance will shift, and so will the responsibility. As IPv6 becomes the predominant protocol on the Internet, the remaining pockets of IPv4 will need to accommodate IPv6, not vice versa. I imagine the transition playing out something like the move from rotary dialing to Touch-Tone™; in 1963, when the switch began, Touch-Tone™ was a novelty you had to pay extra for. Now, of course, Touch-Tone™ is the norm (unless you've already moved on to VoIP) and rotary dialing is a curiosity you have to pay your phone company more to accommodate—if they can still handle it at all.

IPv6 and DNS

The exhaustion of the IPv4 address space wasn't unexpected, of course. The Internet Engineering Task Force (IETF) developed IP version 6 in the 1990s largely in anticipation of this day. Likewise, the Domain Name System was extended to accommodate IPv6's longer IP addresses by adding new record types, and new versions of name servers, including BIND, were released to support those new record types as well as the use of IPv6 to transport queries and responses. At this point, all but ancient BIND name servers support IPv6, though in most cases that support isn't configured or used. We've just been waiting patiently for the protocol to catch on!

The ABCs of IPv6 Addresses

The most widely known aspect of IPv6, and really the only one that matters to DNS, is the length of the IPv6 address: 128 bits, four times as long as IPv4's 32-bit address. The preferred representation of an IPv6 address is eight groups of as many as four hexadecimal digits, separated by colons. For example:

    2001:0db8:0123:4567:89ab:cdef:0123:4567

The first group, or *quartet*, of hex digits (2001, in this example) represents the most significant (or highest-order) sixteen bits of the address. In binary terms, 2001 is equivalent to 0010000000000001.

Groups of digits that begin with one or more zeros don't need to be padded to four places, so you can also write the previous address as:

    2001:db8:123:4567:89ab:cdef:123:4567

Each group must contain at least one digit, though, unless you're using the :: notation. The :: notation allows you to compress sequential groups of zeros. This comes in handy when you're specifying just an IPv6 prefix. For example:

    2001:db8:dead:beef::

specifies the first 64 bits of an IPv6 address as *2001:db8:dead:beef* and the remaining 64 as zeros.

You can also use :: at the beginning of an IPv6 address to specify a suffix. For example, the IPv6 loopback address is commonly written as:

    ::1

or 127 bits of zero followed by a single one bit. You can even use :: in the middle of an address as shorthand for contiguous groups of zeros:

    2001:db8:dead:beef::1

You can use the :: shorthand only once in an address, since more than one would be ambiguous.

IPv6 prefixes are specified in a format similar to IPv4's CIDR notation. As many bits of the prefix as are significant are expressed in the standard IPv6 notation, followed by a slash and a decimal count of exactly how many significant bits there are. So the following four prefix specifications are equivalent (though obviously not equivalently terse):

```
2001:db8:dead:beef:0000:00f1:0000:0000/96
2001:db8:dead:beef:0:f1:0:0/96
2001:db8:dead:beef::f1:0:0/96
2001:db8:dead:beef:0:f1::/96
```

IPv6 is similar to IPv4 in that it supports variable-length network masks, and addresses are divided into network and host portions. However, in IPv6, there are recommended network masks for networks and subnets: the first 48 bits of an IPv6 address should identify a particular end site and a 64-bit prefix should identify one of up to 65,536 subnetworks at the site identified by the "parent" 48-bit prefix. As of this writing, all global unicast IPv6 addresses on the Internet (addresses that are unique and globally routable) have prefixes that begin with the binary value 001 (equivalent to 2000::/3). These are assigned by Regional Internet Registries (RIRs) and Internet service providers. The prefix itself may be hierarchical, with an RIR responsible for allocating higher-order bits to various ISPs, and ISPs responsible for allocating the lowest-order bits of the prefix to its customers.

After the end-site prefix, unicast IPv6 addresses typically contain another 16 bits that identify the particular subnetwork within an end site, called the *subnet ID*. The remaining bits of the address identify a particular network interface and are referred to as the *interface ID*.

Here's a diagram that shows how these parts fit together:

```
|        48 bits         | 16 bits  |           64 bits          |
+------------------------+----------+----------------------------+
|         prefix         | subnet ID|        interface ID        |
+------------------------+----------+----------------------------+
/                          \
|                           +--------------------------------\
| 3bits | 9bits | 12-20bits |        16-24bits          |
+-------+-------+-----------+---------------------------+
| IETF  | IANA  |    RIR    |       RIR or ISP          |
+-------+-------+-----------+---------------------------+
```

As you can see in the diagram, the 48-bit prefix is made up of several parts. As previously mentioned, the first three bits are assigned by IETF to indicate "Global Unicast Space." The next nine bits are assigned by IANA to a particular RIR (for example, 2620::/12 is assigned to ARIN, the American Registry for Internet Numbers). The RIR then assigns prefixes to ISPs and end users ranging from 24 to 48 bits (the RIR controls between 12 and 36 bits). Finally, in an ISP's address space, the ISP can assign the bits after its RIR-assigned prefix up to the /48 allocated to each customer end site.

Coincidentally, Movie University just arranged to get IPv6 connectivity from our ISP. The ISP assigned us a /48-sized IPv6 network, 2001:db8:cafe::/48, which we'll subnet using the scheme just described into /64-sized subnetworks.

What's this fe80:: address?

If you're poking around on a Unix or Linux system with *ifconfig, netstat* or the like, you may notice that your host's network interfaces already have IPv6 addresses assigned to them, starting with the quartet "fe80." These are link-local scoped addresses, derived automatically from the interfaces' hardware addresses. The link-local scope is significant—you can't access these addresses from anywhere but the local subnet, so don't use them in delegation, *masters* substatements, and the like. Use global unicast addresses assigned to the host instead. You probably shouldn't even use link-local addresses in the configuration of resolvers on the same subnet if there's any chance that those resolvers will move (e.g., if they're on laptops or other mobile devices).

IPv6 Forward and Reverse Mapping

Clearly, DNS's A record won't accommodate IPv6's 128-bit addresses; an A record's record-specific data is a 32-bit address in dotted-octet format.

The IETF came up with a simple solution to this problem, described in RFC 1886. A new type of address record, AAAA, was used to store a 128-bit IPv6 address, and a new IPv6 reverse-mapping domain, *ip6.int*, was introduced. This solution was straightforward enough to implement in BIND 4. Unfortunately, not everyone liked the simple solution, so they came up with a much more complicated one. This solution introduced the new A6 and DNAME records and required a complete overhaul of the BIND name server to implement. Then, after much acrimonious debate, the IETF decided that the new A6/DNAME scheme involved too much overhead, was prone to failure, and was of unproven usefulness. At least temporarily, they moved the RFC that describes A6 records off the IETF standards track to experimental status, deprecated the use of DNAME records in reverse-mapping zones, and trotted old RFC 1886 back out. Everything old is new again.

For now, the AAAA record is the way to handle IPv6 forward mapping. The use of *ip6.int* is deprecated, however, mostly for political reasons; it's been replaced by *ip6.arpa*.

AAAA and ip6.arpa

The AAAA (pronounced "quad A," not "ahh!") record, described in RFC 1886, is a simple address record with record-specific data that's four times as long as an A record, hence the four As in the record type. The AAAA record takes as its record-specific data the textual format of an IPv6 address, exactly as described earlier. So for example, you'd see AAAA records like this one:

```
ipv6-host    IN    AAAA    2001:db8:1:2:3:4:567:89ab
```

As you can see, it's perfectly okay to use shortcuts in the IPv6 address, including dropping leading zeroes from quartets and replacing one or more contiguous quartets of all zeroes with ::.

RFC 1886 also established *ip6.int*, now replaced by *ip6.arpa*, a new reverse-mapping name space for IPv6 addresses. Each level of subdomain under *ip6.arpa* represents four bits of the 128-bit address, encoded as a hexadecimal digit just like in the record-specific data of the AAAA record. The least significant (lowest-order) bits appear at the far left of the domain name. Unlike the format of IPv6 addresses in AAAA records, omitting leading zeros is not allowed, so there are always 32 hexadecimal digits and 32 levels of subdomain below *ip6.arpa* in a domain name corresponding to a full IPv6 address. The domain name that corresponds to the address in the previous example is:

```
b.a.9.8.7.6.5.0.4.0.0.0.3.0.0.0.2.0.0.0.1.0.0.0.8.b.d.0.1.0.0.2.ip6.arpa.
```

These domain names have PTR records attached, just as the domain names under *in-addr.arpa* do:

```
b.a.9.8.7.6.5.0.4.0.0.0.3.0.0.0.2.0.0.0.1.0.0.0.0.8.b.d.1.0.0.2.ip6.arpa.  IN  PTR
mash.ip6.movie.edu.
```

Adding AAAA Records to Forward-Mapping Zones

A and AAAA records can coexist side-by-side in any forward-mapping zone. So, for example, if your host has both an IPv4 and an IPv6 address (commonly called a "dual-stack" host), you can attach both A and AAAA records to its domain name:

```
suckerpunch    IN    A     192.249.249.111
               IN    AAAA  2001:db8:cafe:f9::d3
```

However, you should be careful with that configuration, at least for the time being. Some current resolvers will always look up AAAA records before A records, even if the host running the resolver lacks the ability to communicate with all IPv6 addresses (for example, the host only has a link-local IPv6 address, or uses some transition technology that gives it limited IPv6 connectivity). If you attach both A and AAAA records to a single domain name, as in the example above, a user of one of these broken resolvers would need to wait for his connection to the IPv6 address to time out before successfully connecting to the IPv4 address, which could take as long as a few minutes (see "Handling Broken Resolvers" in Chapter 2 for a mechanism to help you deal with this).

Until these broken resolvers are fixed, it's prudent to attach A and AAAA records to different domain names, at least for hosts offering services:

```
suckerpunch      IN   A     192.249.249.111
suckerpunch-v6   IN   AAAA 2001:db8:cafe:f9::d3
```

If you like the aesthetics better, you can use "v6" as a label in the domain name instead of as a suffix to the hostname:

```
suckerpunch.v6   IN   AAAA 2001:db8:cafe:f9::d3
```

Note that this doesn't require that you create a new subzone called *v6.movie.edu*; a subdomain in the same zone will do nicely.

IPv6 Reverse-Mapping Zones

If you use the standard IPv6 subnetting scheme shown in the diagram in "The ABCs of IPv6 Addresses", the reverse-mapping zones that correspond to your subnets will have 18 labels. For example, the subnet that *suckerpunch.v6.movie.edu* is on, 2001:db8:cafe:f9::/64, would correspond to the reverse-mapping zone *9.f.0.0.e.f.a.c.8.b.d.0.1.0.0.2.ip6.arpa*. Remember that DNS is case-insensitive, so we could also have called the zone *9.F.0.0.E.F.A.C.8.B.D.0.1.0.0.2.IP6.ARPA* or even *9.F.0.0.e.F.a.C.8.b.D.0.1.0.0.2.iP6.aRpA*, if we'd been feeling punchy. They all would have handled reverse mapping of IPv6 addresses just as well.

As with IPv4 reverse-mapping zones, IPv6 reverse-mapping zones mostly contain PTR records. And as with any zone, they must contain one SOA record and one or more NS records. Here's what the beginning of that zone looks like:

```
$TTL 1d
@   IN   SOA   terminator.movie.edu.    hostmaster.movie.edu.    (
    2011030800          ; Serial number
    1h                  ; Refresh (1 hour)
    15m                 ; Retry (15 minutes)
    30d                 ; Expire (30 days)
    10m )               ; Negative-caching TTL (10 minutes)

    IN   NS   terminator.movie.edu.
    IN   NS   wormhole.movie.edu.

3.d.0.0.0.0.0.0.0.0.0.0.0.0.0.0   PTR   suckerpunch.v6.movie.edu.
4.d.0.0.0.0.0.0.0.0.0.0.0.0.0.0   PTR   super8.v6.movie.edu.
```

Here's hoping that most of your hosts will use dynamic update to register their own AAAA and PTR records, or else you're going to wear out the period key on your keyboard.

If you're going to add a lot of PTR records to an IPv6 reverse-mapping zone by hand, it's a good idea to make liberal use of the $ORIGIN control statement. For example, you could rewrite those last two PTR records as:

```
$ORIGIN 0.0.0.0.0.0.0.0.0.0.0.0.0.0.0.9.f.0.0.e.f.a.c.8.b.d.0.1.0.0.2.ip6.arpa.
3.d       PTR     suckerpunch.v6.movie.edu.
4.d       PTR     super8.v6.movie.edu.
```

The *zone* statement we added to the *named.conf* file on *terminator* to configure it as the primary name server for the reverse-mapping zone looks like this:

```
zone "9.f.0.0.e.f.a.c.8.b.d.0.1.0.0.2.ip6.arpa" {
    type master;
    file "db.2001:db8:cafe:f9";
};
```

Of course, you can name the zone data file whatever you like, but I suggest embedding the subnet's prefix in there somewhere.

 It's probably best to avoid the use of the $GENERATE control statement in IPv6 reverse-mapping zones. Figuring out the right syntax to use to generate PTR records for such zones is tricky, and it's easy to create so many PTR records that you can cause your name server to run out of memory.

Delegation and Reverse-Mapping Zones

You handle delegation with IPv6 reverse-mapping zones just as you would with IPv4 reverse-mapping zones—except it's easier in one important respect. Those of you unfortunate enough to employ IPv4 subnet masks that don't end on an octet boundary (e.g. /8, /16, and /24) wind up with either more than one reverse-mapping zone per subnet or multiple subnets per reverse-mapping zone. Those of you with subnets smaller than a /24 may even be forced to follow RFC 2317, which is really unfortunate.

With IPv6's standard subnetting scheme, each subnet can contain a whopping 2^{64} addresses, and you usually get over 65,000 subnets (assuming your ISP or RIR assigns a full /48 to you). Consequently, you probably won't find yourself tempted to try to use a non-aligned subnet mask to make a subnet just large enough to accommodate the connected hosts. You'll create a /48-sized reverse-mapping zone for your entire IPv6 network, and if necessary can delegate /64-sized subdomains from it.

For Movie University's /48, 2001:db8:cafe::/48, the corresponding reverse-mapping zone is *e.f.a.c.8.b.d.0.1.0.0.2.ip6.arpa*. If we needed to delegate the 2001:db8:cafe:f9::/64 subnet, introduced earlier, to a different set of name servers, we could add delegation like so:

```
$TTL 1d
@   IN   SOA   terminator.movie.edu.     hostmaster.movie.edu.     (
    2011030800        ; Serial number
    1h                ; Refresh (1 hour)
    15m               ; Retry (15 minutes)
    30d               ; Expire (30 days)
    10m )             ; Negative-caching TTL (10 minutes)
```

```
            IN   NS    terminator.movie.edu.
            IN   NS    wormhole.movie.edu.

    9.f.0.0  IN   NS    adjustmentbureau.movie.edu.
            IN   NS    rango.movie.edu.
```

Of course, no glue addresses are necessary, because the domain names of the name servers aren't below the delegation point.

Built-In Empty Reverse-Mapping Zones

There are quite a few IPv6 addresses and networks that serve special purposes. For example, IPv6, like IPv4, has an unspecified address (used by uninitialized network interfaces) and a loopback address, as well as networks for link-local addresses and more. The latest versions of BIND 9 include built-in empty versions of the reverse-mapping zones that correspond to these addresses and networks. The zones are empty so that your local BIND name server will respond to any queries to reverse map these addresses immediately with a negative answer, without forwarding that query off to the Internet to another name server just to get the same negative answer or no answer at all.

The table below lists the built-in reverse-mapping zones, the functions of the addresses and networks they map to, and the rough equivalent in IPv4:

Reverse-mapping Zone Name	Function	IPv4 Equivalent
0.0.0.0.0.0.0.0.0.0.0.0.0.0.0.0.0.0.0.0.0.0.0.0.0.0.0.0.0.0.0.0.ip6.arpa	Unspecified IPv6 address	0.0.0.0
1.0.0.0.0.0.0.0.0.0.0.0.0.0.0.0.0.0.0.0.0.0.0.0.0.0.0.0.0.0.0.0.ip6.arpa	IPv6 Loopback Address	127.0.0.1
8.b.d.0.1.0.0.2.ip6.arpa	IPv6 Documentation Network	192.0.2/24
d.f.ip6.arpa	Unique Local Addresses	10/8, etc. (RFC 1918)
8.e.f.ip6.arpa	Link-Local Addresses	169.254/16
9.e.f.ip6.arpa	Link-Local Addresses	169.254/16
a.e.f.ip6.arpa	Link-Local Addresses	169.254/16
b.e.f.ip6.arpa	Link-Local Addresses	169.254/16

BIND is smart enough to notice if you've already configured your own version of one of these reverse-mapping zones (even if the zone isn't an authoritative zone, such as a forward or stub zone), so you can easily override BIND's empty zones. To disable individual built-in empty zones without creating explicit *zone* statements for them, use the *disable-empty-zone* substatement, which takes as an argument the domain name of the zone to disable:

```
options {
    disable-empty-zone "d.f.ip6.arpa";
};
```

To disable all built-in empty zones, you can use the *empty-zones-enable* substatement. By default, of course, they're enabled, so

```
options {
    empty-zones-enable no;
};
```

will disable them. You can use *disable-empty-zone* and *empty-zones-enable* as either *options* or *view* substatements.

CHAPTER 2

BIND on IPv6

Modern BIND 9 name servers include complete support for IPv6, which means not only handling queries that ask for the IPv6 addresses of a given domain name, but also responding to those queries over IPv6, as well as querying other name servers over IPv6.

Listening for Queries

By default, BIND 9 name servers won't listen for queries that arrive on an IPv6 interface. To tell the name server to listen on an IPv6 interface, use the *listen-on-v6* substatement. The simplest form of this substatement is:

```
options {
    listen-on-v6 { any; };
};
```

which instructs the name server to listen for queries on any IPv6 network interfaces configured on the host. If you need to be more selective, you can specify a particular interface or particular interfaces:

```
options {
    listen-on-v6 { 2001:db8:cafe:1::1; 2001:db8:cafe:2::1; };
};
```

You can even negate entries in the list and specify entire networks, in which case the name server will listen on any interface on the matching network. If you need your name server to listen on a port other than 53 (the default), specify it immediately after *listen-on-v6*. Here's an example that incorporates all of these:

```
options {
    listen-on-v6 port 5353 { !2001:db8:cafe:1::1; 2001:db8:cafe::/64; };
};
```

This configures the name server to listen on port 5353 on all interfaces with IPv6 addresses on the network 2001:db8:cafe::/64 (that is, the Movie U. IPv6 network) except the address 2001:db8:cafe:1::1.

If you need to have your name server listen on multiple ports at the same time, just use multiple *listen-on-v6* substatements. You can only use *listen-on-v6* as an *options* substatement, since it controls the behavior of the entire *named* process.

Sending Queries

Once you've configured a name server to listen on an IPv6 interface, the name server will automatically query other name servers over IPv6 when necessary. The source IP address of these queries will depend on which interface the route to the queried name server points through. To change this behavior, use the *query-source-v6* substatement.

query-source-v6 uses a syntax that is—somewhat frustratingly—different from that of *listen-on-v6*. The name server's default behavior, using whichever source IPv6 address a route points through and whichever query port suits it, is equivalent to this substatement:

```
options {
    query-source-v6 address * port *;
};
```

To tell the name server to use a particular address, simply replace the * after the *address* keyword with a single IPv6 address, like so:

```
options {
    query-source-v6 address 2001:db8:cafe:1::1;
};
```

As with *listen-on-v6*, *query-source-v6* can only be used as an *options* substatement.

You can also specify that the name server use a particular source port in outgoing queries—but you shouldn't. This defeats the name server's query port randomization, which is a very important weapon against cache-poisoning attacks.

More on Query Port Randomization

Ever since the discovery of the Kaminsky vulnerability, BIND name servers have sent queries from random ports to make it more difficult to spoof responses to those queries. With random query ports, a would-be spoofer must guess which port to send a spoofed response to. And by default, BIND 9 chooses its random query ports from a very large pool: from port 1024 to port 65535.

If you need to tell the name server not to use a particular query port—for example, because certain ports are blocked by your firewall—use the *avoid-v6-udp-ports* substatement, which takes a list of ports as its argument:

```
options {
    avoid-v6-udp-ports { 1024; 1025; };
};
```

You can also specify the list of ports to avoid as a range:

```
options {
    avoid-v6-udp-ports { range 1024 1025; };
};
```

If for whatever reason you need to restrict the range of ports BIND uses to one smaller than the default, use the *use-v6-udp-ports* substatement, which takes the range as an argument:

```
options {
    use-v6-udp-ports { range 1024 16727; };
};
```

Again, be very careful, since restricting the range too much will limit the effectiveness of query port randomization.

Forcing the Use of a Particular Protocol

Occasionally, you may want to force a name server not to use IPv4 or IPv6 despite the fact that the host it's running on has dual stacks. For example, you may know that the host isn't capable of reaching the entire IPv6 Internet because of limitations in the transition technology you use. In situations like this, you can tell the name server to use only IPv4 or only IPv6 with the –4 and –6 command-line options, respectively.

```
% named -4
```

tells the name server to use only IPv4, while

```
% named -6
```

obviously, tells the name server to use only IPv6.

IPv6 Masters and Slaves

Of course, BIND supports zone transfers over IPv6, too. To configure a slave name server to transfer a zone from its master using IPv6, just specify the master's IPv6 address in the zone's *masters* substatement:

```
zone "movie.edu" {
    type slave;
    masters { 2001:db8:cafe:1::1; };
    file "bak.movie.edu";
};
```

To make this more readable, I suggest using the new *masters* statement. *masters* lets you assign a name to a list of master name servers, and then refer to that name in *zone* statements. Even if the list consists of just a single master name server, giving it a name will make it much easier to identify:

```
masters terminator.movie.edu { 2001:db8:cafe:1::1; };

zone "movie.edu" {
    type slave;
```

```
        masters { terminator.movie.edu; };
        file "bak.movie.edu";
};
```

If you want to specify a TSIG key or even an alternate port on the master name server to transfer from, you can specify those in the *masters* statement:

```
masters terminator-and-wormhole {
    2001:db8:cafe:1::1 key tsig.movie.edu;
    2001:db8:cafe:2::1 port 5353 key tsig.movie.edu;
};
```

You can even use names defined in *masters* statements with stub zones.

Note that *masters* is a top-level statement: you can't use it inside an *options* or *view* statement.

Other IPv6 Zone Transfer Controls

As you'd expect, given the thoroughness of the good folks at ISC who develop BIND, there are also IPv6 equivalents of the *transfer-source* and *notify-source* substatements, called, not surprisingly, *transfer-source-v6* and *notify-source-v6*. These instruct the name server to use particular IPv6 source addresses when initiating zone transfers from master name servers or when sending NOTIFY messages to slave name servers. These can be useful when, for example, a master name server only allows zone transfers initiated from a particular IPv6 address but the slave has multiple IPv6 addresses[*], or when a slave only knows its master name server by a particular IPv6 address (and therefore ignores NOTIFY messages from other IPv6 addresses the master may have).

The default, of course, is to use the IPv6 address of whichever interface the route to the master or slave points through, which is the same as:

```
options {
    transfer-source-v6 *;
    notify-source-v6 *;
};
```

To initiate zone transfers or send NOTIFY messages only from a particular IPv6 address, simply replace * with that address, like this:

```
options {
    transfer-source-v6 2001:db8:cafe:1::1;
    notify-source-v6 2001:db8:cafe:1::1;
};
```

---

[*] But they really ought to use TSIG to secure zone transfers, not IP address-based ACLs.

IPv6 Networks and Addresses in ACLs

To support IPv6, access control lists (ACLs) were extended to allow the specification of IPv6 addresses. Specifying IPv6 addresses in ACLs works as you'd expect it to:

```
acl Movie-U {
    2001:db8:cafe::/48;
};

acl campus-subnets {
    2001:db8:cafe:1::/64;
    2001:db8:cafe:2::/64;
};
```

You can, of course, mix IPv4 and IPv6 in the same ACL:

```
acl terminator {
    2001:db8:cafe:1::1;
    192.249.249.1;
};
```

And you can negate entries, too, to prevent matches:

```
acl all-subnet-but-terminator {
    !2001:db8:cafe:1::1;
    2001:db8:cafe:1::/64;
};
```

The built-in *localhost* and *localnets* ACLs have also been enhanced: *localhost* now includes all of the host's IPv6 addresses as well as its IPv4 addresses. (Note that this typically includes both a link-local address and a global unicast address on a name server configured to run over IPv6.) *localnets* includes IPv4 and IPv6 networks connected to the host, providing the operating system supports determining the prefix length of the host's IPv6 addresses. If it doesn't, *localnets* includes locally connected IPv4 *networks* but just the host's IPv6 *addresses*.

Especially with IPv6, I encourage you to define and use ACLs with intuitive names to make your *named.conf* files more readable. There's a tremendous difference between this:

```
allow-query {
    192.249.249/24;
    192.253.253/24;
    2001:db8:cafe:1::/64;
    2001:db8:cafe:2::/64;
};
```

and this:

```
allow-query {
    movie-u-internal-networks;
};
```

Registering IPv6 Name Servers

Once you've set up an IPv6 name server that's authoritative for one or more zones, you may want to add the new IPv6 address to those zones' delegation information. That will require that your parent support registration of IPv6 addresses for name servers. Almost all top-level domains, such as *com*, *net*, and *org* and most large country-code top-level domains, such as *uk* and *de*, support IPv6 addresses for name servers. In most cases, however, you don't deal directly with the administrators of these domains, but rather work through an intermediary called a *registrar*. Unfortunately, not all registrars support registration of IPv6 addresses. If yours doesn't, you may have no choice but to transfer your zones to a registrar that does, or at least threaten to if they don't get their act together.

The actual process you use to register a name server's IPv6 address varies depending on the registrar, but most good registrars provide reasonably intuitive web-based interfaces for managing delegation information and allow you to simply enter an IPv6 address there.

If your parent zone is managed by someone else in your organization—say a network administrator at your company's corporate headquarters—ask them how they'd like the new address submitted. It may be as easy as sending them email.

For the time being, while IPv6 is still catching on, make sure that you register both IPv4 and IPv6 addresses for your name servers. If you don't have any IPv4–speaking name servers, most recursive name servers on the Internet won't be able to resolve any of your domain names.

Delegating to IPv6 Name Servers

If you manage a parent zone (that is, you're the network administrator at your company's corporate headquarters mentioned earlier), the administrators of your subzones may ask you to add IPv6 addresses to their delegation. Doing so is straightforward.

Say the network administrator of our computer-generated imagery department, *cgi.movie.edu*, has just set up a new IPv6 network and wants us to add his name servers' new IPv6 addresses to his delegation. Currently, his delegation looks like this:

```
cgi.movie.edu.          IN    NS    avatar.cgi.movie.edu.
cgi.movie.edu.          IN    NS    tron.cgi.movie.edu.

avatar.cgi.movie.edu.         IN    A     192.249.249.169
tron.cgi.movie.edu.           IN    A     192.253.253.169
```

He's just set up the IPv6 subnets 2001:db8:cafe:10::/64 and 2001:db8:cafe:11::/64, so after adding AAAA records for the two hosts, the delegation looks like this:

```
cgi.movie.edu.          IN    NS    avatar.cgi.movie.edu.
cgi.movie.edu.          IN    NS    tron.cgi.movie.edu.
```

```
avatar.cgi.movie.edu.        IN    A     192.249.249.169
                             IN    AAAA  2001:db8:cafe:10::2
tron.cgi.movie.edu.          IN    A     192.253.253.169
                             IN    AAAA  2001:db8:cafe:11::2
```

It's worth reiterating here that glue A or AAAA records are necessary in delegation only when a subdomain is delegated to a name server that ends in the name of the subdomain (as *tron.cgi.movie.edu* ends in *cgi.movie.edu*). If that's not true, glue records aren't needed.

Server Statements for IPv6 Name Servers

If you need to tweak the way your name server communicates with a particular remote name server, you use the *server* statement. The server statement now supports IPv6 addresses, too, so if you wanted to tell your name server to use the TSIG key *movie.edu.key* when communicating with *terminator.movie.edu* over IPv6, you could use the following server statement:

```
server 2001:db8:cafe:1::1 {
    keys { movie.edu.key; };
};
```

And remember that the server statement now (since at least BIND 9.5.0) accepts the specification of an entire network as an argument, so you can configure how your name server communicates with a whole set of name servers. For example, to tell your name server not to query any of the name servers on the Movie U. IPv6 network, you could use this server statement:

```
server 2001:db8:cafe::/48 {
    bogus yes;
};
```

But why would you ever want to do that?

For a more complete list of *server* substatements, see *DNS and BIND*.

Special Considerations

Handling "Monolingual" Name Servers

For the foreseeable future, we'll run both the IPv4 and IPv6 protocols in parallel on the Internet. While today, the vast majority of zones are served by name servers with only IPv4 connectivity, some day—hopefully sooner rather than later—we'll see zones served only by IPv6 name servers. Either kind of zone introduces an interoperability challenge, though: how can a recursive name server with only IPv6 connectivity resolve a domain name in a zone served only by IPv4 name servers? And what about the converse?

BIND 9 allows you to configure a sort of "protocol forwarder" called a *dual-stack server* for these poor monolingual recursors. When a recursor needs to look up data in a zone served only by name servers that don't speak the same protocol, it simply forwards that query to the dual-stack server and waits for a response. (The forwarded query is recursive, otherwise the name server doing the forwarding might receive a referral in reply, which wouldn't help much.)

The basic syntax is similar to that used to configure forwarders:

```
dual-stack-servers { 192.249.249.1; 192.249.249.3; };
```

You can also specify the dual-stack servers by domain name, which is a nice change:

```
dual-stack-servers {
    terminator.movie.edu;
    wormhole.movie.edu;
};
```

Just make sure your name server can resolve the domain names of the dual-stack servers to addresses with the one protocol it speaks.

As a best practice, however, it's a good idea to run your name servers on dual-stack hosts whenever possible and to use dual-stack-servers only when you have no other choice.

Handling Broken Resolvers

Including support for IPv6 in a resolver is laudable. Preferring IPv6 addresses when they're available is admirably progressive, too. But some resolvers will look up AAAA records even though the underlying operating system can't really use them. Maybe the host uses a tunneling configuration that gives it limited IPv6 connectivity, for example. When the resolver returns the IPv6 address, and some client software tries to connect to it, it can take several minutes for the client to fall back to IPv4. Worse, the software can incur this delay for every connection it makes—once for each image that appears on a web page, for example.

Thankfully, these situations are fairly rare. Estimates from Google and Yahoo! suggest that these resolvers run on between 0.05% to 0.078% of hosts on the Internet. But while that may not sound like a lot, when you're dealing with a user base as large as theirs, it represents hundreds of thousands of users.

BIND versions 9.7.0 and later include a filtering mechanism for accommodating these resolvers. Basically, the mechanism decides whether or not to return AAAA records to a resolver based on the protocol over which the resolver sent its query. If the query arrived over IPv6, that's proof enough that the resolver—and the host it runs on—has IPv6 connectivity. If the query arrived over IPv4, though, the filter tells the name server to lie and claim (for the resolver's own protection, of course) that no AAAA records exist even for domain names that really do own them. Presumably the resolver then goes on to request plain old A records.

This mechanism is somewhat controversial. Many members of the DNS community don't like the idea of lying to resolvers. Moreover, lying can break DNSSEC validation. So the Internet Systems Consortium, which develops BIND, makes you jump through an extra hoop to use the feature: you need to compile the name server with the *-enable-filter-aaaa* option. The implicit message is, "Don't use this unless you know what you're doing."

If compiled with that option, the name server will let you specify the *filter-aaaa-on-v4* *options* substatement, which takes a simple *yes* or *no* as an argument:

```
options {
    filter-aaaa-on-v4 yes;
};
```

You can also use *filter-aaaa-on-v4* as a *view* substatement, to apply only to that view.

By default, *filter-aaaa-on-v4* doesn't apply to queries with the DNSSEC OK (DO) bit set, because those suggest that the querier may perform DNSSEC validation. To override this, use *break-dnssec* as the argument:

```
options {
    filter-aaaa-on-v4 break-dnssec;
};
```

To apply filtering only to a subset of queriers, you can use the *filter-aaaa options* (and *view*) substatement, which allows you to specify the addresses of queriers whose responses should be filtered:

```
options {
    filter-aaaa-on-v4 yes;
    filter-aaaa { 192.249.249/24; };
};
```

Limiting the filter (if you use it at all) is a good precaution, since filtering can have unwanted side effects. For example, imagine an IPv6-only resolver configured to query a dual-stack recursive name server. If the recursive name server sent IPv4 queries to an authoritative name server that did filtering, it would always be told that no AAAA records existed, which would render the resolver unable to resolve any IPv6 addresses!

rndc and IPv6

rndc, the remote name daemon controller, can now communicate with a BIND name server over IPv6. This usually requires configuration on both the client (i.e., *rndc*) side and the server (*named*) side.

By default, the name server will only accept connections from *rndc* on the host's IPv4 and IPv6 loopback addresses, 127.0.0.1 and ::1, respectively. To tell the name server to listen on all of the host's IPv6 addresses, specify the IPv6 wildcard address, ::, in the *control* statement:

```
controls {
    inet ::
    allow { localnets; }
    keys { rndc-key; };
};
```

You can also specify a single address to listen on:

```
controls {
    inet 2001:db8:cafe:1::1
    allow { localnets; }
    keys { rndc-key; };
};
```

Though not required, it's always a good idea to limit incoming connections to a small set of addresses using an IP address-based ACL, and it's critical to use a key to secure the control channel.

To tell *rndc* to connect to a host's IPv6 address, you can specify the address as the argument to the *-s* option:

```
% rndc -s 2001:db8:cafe:1::1 reload
```

Of course, if there's a domain name that points to that address, you can use that as the option argument instead.

CHAPTER 3

Resolver Configuration

Configuring a resolver to query a name server over IPv6 is a piece of cake—assuming the resolver supports IPv6! You can just plug the IPv6 address of a recursive name server into the resolver. On a Unix-ish operating system, that's usually done in the *resolv.conf* file with a *nameserver* directive:

```
nameserver 2001:db8:cafe:1::1
```

If the resolver is on the same host as a recursive name server, you can use the IPv6 loopback address, of course:

```
nameserver ::1
```

Mac OS X

With Mac OS X, resolver configuration is done in System Preferences. Click on System Preferences, then on *Network* (under the Internet & Wireless category). To configure the name servers you use when connected via AirPort, click on AirPort in the list of network interfaces on the left, then click on the Advanced... button at the lower right. In the window that appears, click on the DNS tab. The resulting window should look like this:

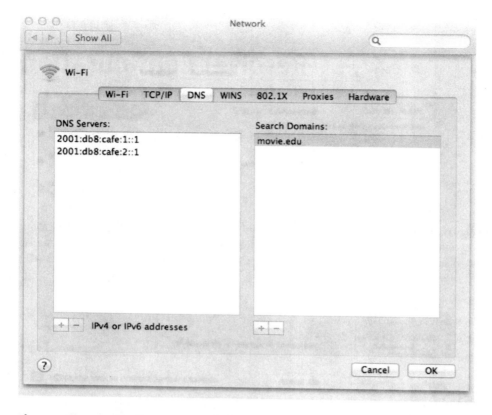

If your computer has been assigned a list of name servers by a DHCP server, you may find the DNS Servers: section populated. You can override this list by clicking the + button below the list, though. Enter one or more IPv6 addresses to query the name servers' IPv6 addresses.

To configure the name servers you use when connected to the Internet via another network interface, such as your Mac's Ethernet interface, simply choose Ethernet from the Network panel.

Windows

With Windows 7, start the Control Panel. Click on Network and Internet, then on Network and Sharing Center. Find the Local Area Connection and click on it. The Local Area Connection Properties window should appear. It looks like this:

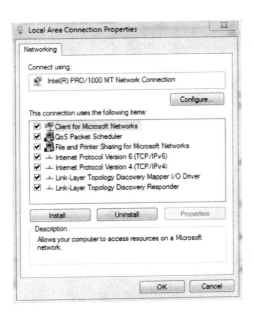

Click on Internet Protocol Version 6 (TCP/IPv6); the Internet Protocol Version 6 (TCP/IPv6) Properties window will appear:

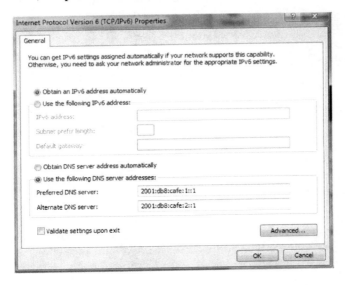

If you click on Use the following DNS server addresses, you can specify the IPv6 addresses of up to two recursive name servers.

As with Mac OS X, to configure the name servers your resolver queries when using a different network interface, simply choose that interface instead of Local Area Connection.

After reconfiguring your resolver to use IPv6, it's a good idea to verify that DNS resolution still works with a tool such as *dig* or *nslookup*. See the chapter on troubleshooting later in this book for details.

Dynamic Resolver Configuration

IPv6 supports several methods for dynamically configuring a host's IP address and other network parameters:

- A "traditional" method, using DHCPv6, the IPv6 version of DHCP
- Stateless Address Autoconfiguration, or SLAAC, in which a host uses Router Advertisements to assemble an IP address appropriate for use on the local network and to determine other network parameters
- A hybrid method, in which a host uses SLAAC for address assignment but DHCPv6 to determine other network parameters

In the first and last methods, resolver configuration involves setting the right DHCPv6 options. In the second, it requires setting up the correct Router Advertisement options.

But wait—how does a host choose whether to use SLAAC, DHCPv6, or both? A router tells it its options with flags in its Router Advertisements:

- The "M" flag, for "Managed Address Configuration," tells hosts that DHCPv6 is available for both address assignment and network parameters (including resolver configuration).
- The "A" flag, for "Autonomous Address Configuration," tells hosts that SLAAC is available for address assignment and network parameters (possibly including resolver configuration).
- The "O" flag, for "Other Stateful Configuration," tells hosts that DHCPv6 is available for network parameters other than address assignment (that is, to be used together with SLAAC in the hybrid method described earlier).

Note that the host has a choice of methods to use and can use more than one. For example, a router may advertise the availability of both SLAAC and DHCPv6 for address assignment, and a host may get one IPv6 address using SLAAC and another using DHCPv6. A host may also receive resolver configuration from both methods, and then merge them. Confusing, eh?

Resolver Configuration Using DHCPv6

IPv6 supports dynamic configuration of hosts using DHCPv6, and naturally you can use DHCPv6 to configure a resolver. DHCPv6 has new resolver configuration options, though—you can't use the same old DHCPv4 options to configure your resolver over DHCPv6. The new options are:

Option Number	ISC Option Name	Option Argument
23	dhcp6.name-servers	Comma-separated list of IPv6 addresses
24	dhcp6.domain-search	Comma-separated list of domain names

And here's a snippet from an ISC DHCP server's *dhcpd.conf* file to show you how the options are set:

```
option dhcp6.name-servers 2001:db8:cafe:1::1, 2001:db8:cafe:2::1;
option dhcp6.domain-search "cgi.movie.edu","movie.edu";
```

The ability to set a search list via DHCP is new; while RFC 3397 introduced a DHCPv4 option to do that back in 2002, it was never widely supported by DHCP clients. DHCPv6 has supported configuration of the search list from the beginning, though, so all DHCPv6 clients should support it.

There's another change in DHCPv6 worth mentioning. In IPv6, DHCP comes in two flavors: stateless and stateful. Stateful DHCPv6 is like DHCP on IPv4: a DHCP client can start with nothing but a MAC address and have an IP address plus other network configuration assigned. But stateless DHCPv6 is new and supports the hybrid method of configuring network stacks: a DHCP client that already has an IP address (e.g., assigned using SLAAC) can retrieve network configuration *excluding address assignment* (which it doesn't need) from a DHCPv6 server.

Resolver Configuration Using Router Advertisements

Router Advertisements originally didn't contain any resolver configuration parameters, so although hosts could use SLAAC to configure most of their network stacks, they couldn't configure their resolvers. For that, they needed to use stateless DHCPv6, which could provide the IPv6 addresses of recursive name servers, as well as other DNS-related parameters, such as a search list, as described in the last section. But this required that every IPv6 subnet be served by a DHCPv6 server, in many cases solely to provide resolver configuration.

Then RFC 6106 extended Router Advertisements to support the specification of the IPv6 addresses of recursive name servers as well as a DNS search list, eliminating the need for a DHCPv6 server in many cases.

The Router Advertisement option used to configure a resolver's name servers is called RDNSS, for Recursive DNS Server. The option for configuring a resolver's search list is called DNSSL, for DNS Search List. As the name suggests, Router Advertisements are sent by routers, so you would usually configure the options on those routers. And, of course, the particular syntax required would vary depending on the make of routers you ran.

I write "would" because RFC 6106 is very new (published in November 2010), so not much gear supports it yet, though there's somewhat more support for RFC 5006, a precursor to RFC 6106. (RFC 5006 introduced support for the RDNSS option but didn't include a way to set a search list.) On the server side, Linux and various BSD operating systems have at least some support in *rtadvd*, the Router Advertisement daemon. On the client side, Mac OS X 10.7 ("Lion") is rumored to support RFC 6106.

Here's an example of configuring the RDNSS option in *rtadvd.conf*, the Linux version of *rtadvd*'s configuration file[*]:

```
interface eth0 {
    AdvSendAdvert on;
    prefix 2001:db8:cafe:1::/64 {
        AdvOnLink on;
        AdvAutonomous on;
    };
    rdnss 2001:db8:cafe:1::1 {
    };
};
```

[*] Note that the BSD operating systems use a substantially different syntax.

CHAPTER 4

DNS64

During the (likely very long) transition from IPv4 to IPv6, ISPs and other organizations will implement new networks that only support IPv6. For the foreseeable future, though, clients on those networks will still need access to services (e.g., websites) that don't yet support IPv6. NAT64 and DNS64* are a pair of complementary transition technologies that help provide that access.

NAT64 is a function run on a dual-stack host. A NAT64 server accepts connections from clients that only speak IPv6 and then uses its own IPv4 connectivity to communicate with IPv4-only servers on those clients' behalf, then copies data between the IPv4 and IPv6 connections, effectively "bridging" the IPv4 and IPv6 networks. The clients don't actually realize they're connecting through NAT64—they're led to believe that the IPv4-only servers they want to communicate with support IPv6 and that they're talking directly to them.

How is that misdirection achieved? Through DNS—DNS64, in particular. The IPv6-only clients are configured to use one or more special name servers that support the DNS64 function. When one of these name servers receives a query from a client for AAAA (IPv6 address) records for some domain name, it looks for an answer, as it normally would. If it doesn't find any such records, it tries looking up A records for the same domain name. If it finds one or more A records, it doesn't return them to the client (which can't use them, anyway, and wouldn't accept them, since it asked specifically for AAAA records). It "synthesizes" an equal number of AAAA records from those A records, embedding the 32-bit IPv4 addresses in 128-bit IPv6 addresses. Now the client believes the server supports IPv6 and that it can communicate with it directly.

The client, then, tries to connect to one of these fictional—er, synthesized—IPv6 addresses. How does the NAT64 server intercept this traffic? Easy! The route to the network on which the synthesized IPv6 address lies leads right to the NAT64 server. The NAT64 server terminates the IPv6 connection, extracts the embedded IPv4 address,

---

* NAT64 and DNS64 are pronounced as "NAT six four" and "DNS six four," respectively—not "NAT sixty-four" and "DNS sixty-four."

and connects to the IPv4 server on the IPv6 client's behalf. This process is illustrated in Figure 4-1.

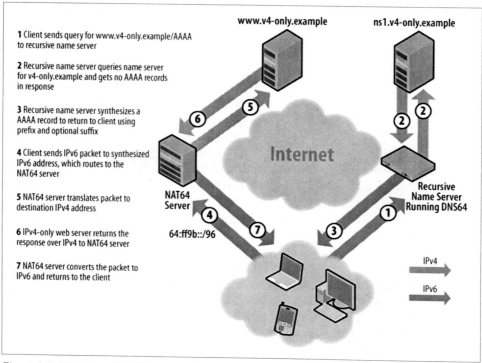

1 Client sends query for www.v4-only.example/AAAA to recursive name server

2 Recursive name server queries name server for v4-only.example and gets no AAAA records in response

3 Recursive name server synthesizes a AAAA record to return to client using prefix and optional suffix

4 Client sends IPv6 packet to synthesized IPv6 address, which routes to the NAT64 server

5 NAT64 server translates packet to destination IPv4 address

6 IPv4-only web server returns the response over IPv4 to NAT64 server

7 NAT64 server converts the packet to IPv6 and returns to the client

Figure 4-1. DNS64 and NAT64 at Work

BIND versions 9.8.0 and later support DNS64 with the *dns64 options* substatement. *dns64* supports the configuration of an IPv6 prefix to which the embedded IPv4 address is appended, as well as an optional suffix that is then appended to the IPv4 address to complete the 128-bit address. (The prefix is often 96 bits long, in which case no suffix is required, or even possible.) Here's a basic example:

```
dns64 64:ff9b::/96 {
    suffix ::;
};
```

::, an all-zeroes suffix, is the default, so you can leave that substatement out if you like.

Now, there are good reasons that you may not want to apply DNS64 to every querier. For instance, you may have a community of dual-stack clients on your network. When asked by an application to find the address of a server, many stub resolvers on dual-stack clients will send AAAA queries before they send A queries. With DNS64 enabled, such clients would never see the A records of IPv4-only servers; DNS64 would always return synthesized AAAA records to them, even though the clients were perfectly capable of using the servers' A records. This, in turn, would shunt traffic through your NAT64 infrastructure unnecessarily.

The *dns64* statement supports a *clients* substatement that allows you to select which clients the DNS64 function applies to. By default, DNS64 applies to all clients; that is:

```
dns64 64:ff9b::/96 {
    clients { any; };
};
```

But you can specify any ACL you like as an argument. Here's an example:

```
dns64 64:ff9b::/96 {
    clients { 2001:db8:cafe:1::/64; };
};
```

As always, it's a good idea to use named ACLs whenever possible for clarity.

There are also IPv4 networks that you may not want mapped into IPv6 addresses by DNS64. For example, if you run a DNS64 function to give your IPv6-only clients access to the IPv4 Internet, you don't want to embed any RFC 1918 addresses that name servers on the Internet might inadvertently return. To avoid that, use the *dns64 mapped* substatement. This *dns64* statement would prevent DNS64 from mapping 10/8 addresses, for example:

```
dns64 64:ff9b://96 {
    mapped { !10/8; any; };
};
```

Of course, RFC 1918 includes more than just 10/8.

 You may notice that I use the prefix 64:ff9b:://96 liberally in my DNS64 examples. That's because that network is reserved for mapping IPv4 addresses into IPv6, and it's the default used by many NAT64 implementations. You can use a different prefix if you prefer, but make sure it matches what's configured on (and routed to) your NAT64 server, and choose it from some private IPv6 address space (there's plenty of it) so it doesn't interfere with routing to real IPv6 destinations. NAT64 prefixes are restricted by RFC to /32s, /40s, /48s, /56s, /64s, or /96s. If you choose a /96, a suffix is superfluous, of course, but other prefix lengths allow the configuration of a suffix (though again, the suffix is optional, and defaults to ::). As with the prefix, make sure your NAT64 server is configured with the same suffix.

Normally, DNS64 only applies to domain names that don't have AAAA records. (If the domain name had one or more AAAA records, the name server would simply have returned them to the IPv6-only client.) But sometimes you may want the name server to ignore AAAA records that contain certain IPv6 addresses and apply DNS64 to a domain name. In that case, you can use the *exclude* substatement, which allows you to specify one or more IPv6 networks or addresses whose presence DNS64 should ignore and synthesize new AAAA records anyway. Here's an example:

```
dns64 64:ff9b::/96 {
    clients { 2001:db8:cafe:1::/64; };
    mapped { !10/8; any; };
    exclude { 64:ff9b::/96; };
};
```

This tells DNS64 to ignore any AAAA records that map to IPv6 addresses on the network 64:ff9b::/96 and to look up A records for those domain names and synthesize new AAAA records instead.

Authoritative Name Servers and DNS64

What I've described so far is DNS64 as performed by a recursive name server, but authoritative name servers can implement DNS64, too. In fact, if you configure your name server to do DNS64 and it's also authoritative for one or more zones, it'll apply DNS64 to queries in those zones by default, too. In this case, the name server synthesizes AAAA records from A records in zones for which it's authoritative. (Of course, it'll only do this if no AAAA records exist for the domain name.)

If you want to restrict DNS64 to recursive queries, you can use the *recursive-only* substatement:

```
dns64 64:ff9b::/96 {
    recursive-only yes;
};
```

The default is to apply DNS64 to both recursive and nonrecursive queries.

Interaction Between DNS64 and DNSSEC

After reading about DNS64, those of you who have already read *DNS and BIND*'s "Security" chapter may object: doesn't the mechanism, *when it's working as designed*, break DNSSEC? Yes, it sure can.

Imagine that a monolingual IPv6 client queries a recursive name server that supports DNS64 for AAAA records attached to a domain name in a signed zone. The recursive name server looks up AAAA records for the domain name and finds none. If the recursive name server is configured to perform DNSSEC validation and has a valid chain of trust to the zone in question, it will cryptographically validate the negative response from the authoritative name server. Surely it can't lie to the client about an answer it has validated?

Actually, it can, and in many cases, the client won't notice at all. That's because most clients don't perform validation themselves, but rely entirely on their recursive name servers for that.

As a safeguard, however, a BIND name server doesn't synthesize a AAAA response if the DNSSEC OK (DO) flag was set in the query. In this case, the client querying the name server could be another name server configured to use it as a forwarder, and *it* might be configured to perform validation. That validation would fail on any synthesized AAAA record.

If you're really hell-bent on rewriting even those responses, you can use the *break-dnssec* substatement:

```
dns64 64:ff9b://96 {
    break-dnssec yes;
};
```

DNS64 and Reverse Mapping

There's one last detail of DNS64 worth mentioning: reverse mapping. If a client using a name server configured to perform DNS64 tries to reverse-map a synthesized IPv6 address, what happens? The name server in question responds with a CNAME record pointing the domain name used to reverse-map the synthesized IPv6 address (the one under *ip6.arpa*) to the domain name corresponding to the embedded IPv4 address (under *in-addr.arpa*). So if an A record pointing to 192.168.0.1 synthesizes a AAAA record pointing to 64:ff9b::192.168.0.1 (or 64:ff9b::c0a8:1—same thing), the CNAME record looks like this:

```
1.0.0.0.8.a.0.c.0.0.0.0.0.0.0.0.0.0.0.0.0.0.b.9.f.f.6.4.0.0.ip6.arpa.    CNAME
1.0.168.192.in-addr.arpa.
```

The result is exactly what you'd want: the synthesized IPv6 address reverse-maps to whichever domain name the embedded IPv4 address maps to!

CHAPTER 5

Troubleshooting

Troubleshooting IPv6-related DNS problems isn't much different from troubleshooting other DNS problems. The main things you need to know are how to specify the IPv6 address of a name server to query and how to forward-map and reverse-map IPv6 addresses. I'll show you how to use both *nslookup* and *dig* to perform these tasks.

There's one important thing to keep in mind with either query tool: they default to using IPv4, which means that whether you type *nslookup terminator.movie.edu* or *dig wormhole.movie.edu*, the program will look up A records (that is, IPv4 addresses). You need to specify AAAA records explicitly to look up IPv6 addresses. Likewise, *nslookup – terminator.movie.edu* will send a query to the name server's IPv4 address, not its IPv6 address. With recent versions of *dig*, *dig @terminator.movie.edu* will query the name server's IPv6 address first, assuming *terminator.movie.edu* owns a AAAA record.

nslookup

First, I'll reiterate something we said in *DNS and BIND*: *nslookup* is not a great troubleshooting tool for a number of reasons. It insulates you from the details of the DNS message and is prone to displaying errors that are unrelated to the query you're interested in, such as an inability to reverse-map the address of the name server it's querying to a domain name. But *nslookup* is more prevalent than my preferred DNS troubleshooting tool, *dig*, so I'm obliged to cover it.

First, to query a name server over IPv6, you'll need to use either *nslookup*'s *server* command or specify the server's IPv6 address on the command line. Most people use *nslookup*'s interactive mode, which you can enter simply by typing *nslookup*:

```
% nslookup
>
```

nslookup displays the > prompt in interactive mode. By default, *nslookup* will read the local host's *resolv.conf* file and query the first name server listed in the file, or if no name server is specified, will try querying a name server on the local host, as the local resolver would. To change to query a different name server over IPv6, use the *server* command:

```
% nslookup
>   server 2001:db8:cafe:1::1
Default server: 2001:db8:cafe:1:1
Address: 2001:db8:cafe:1:1
```

You can also specify the server by its domain name, but if the domain name also points to an IPv4 address, *nslookup* will try to query that:

```
% nslookup
>   server terminator.movie.edu
Default server: terminator.movie.edu
Address: 192.249.249.1
```

Whoops. Look at the Address line. For situations like this, it's a good idea to have a special domain name that points only to the name server's IPv6 address, like *terminator-v6.movie.edu* or *terminator.v6.movie.edu*. Then the *server* command will work nicely:

```
% nslookup
>   server terminator.v6.movie.edu
Default server: terminator.v6.movie.edu
Address: 2001:db8:cafe:1::1
```

 Specifying the name server to query by domain name is a little dangerous, both because the name may not map to the address you expect (as in the example above) and because if you're using a troubleshooting tool such as *nslookup* or *dig*, DNS is probably misbehaving anyway.

The last thing you want is to spend a lot of time troubleshooting a problem only to find that you're not querying the name server you thought you were. So if you do specify the name server to query by name, double-check its address, and if in doubt, specify the name server by address instead.

In *nslookup*'s non-interactive mode, you can specify the server to query after you specify the domain name to look up. For example:

```
% nslookup -type=aaaa suckerpunch.movie.edu. terminator.v6.movie.edu.
```

If you want to specify the server to query but enter interactive mode, just use "-" in place of the domain name to query:

```
% nslookup - terminator.v6.movie.edu.
```

Finally, to forward-map and reverse-map IPv6 addresses, use the query types *aaaa* and *ptr*, respectively. Here's how you'd look up *suckerpunch.movie.edu*'s IPv6 address:

```
% nslookup
> set q=aaaa
> suckerpunch.movie.edu.
Server:        terminator.v6.movie.edu.
Address: 2001:db8:cafe:1::1#53

suckerpunch.movie.edu    has AAAA address 2001:db8:cafe:f9::d3
>
```

And here's how you'd reverse-map the address. Note that you don't need to specify the query type explicitly—*nslookup* is smart enough to recognize the IPv6 address. You also can use the abbreviated form of the IPv6 address, dropping leading zeroes from quartets and using the :: shortcut:

```
% nslookup
> 2001:db8:cafe:f9::d3
Server:         terminator.v6.movie.edu.
Address: 2001:db8:cafe:1::1#53

3.d.0.0.0.0.0.0.0.0.0.0.0.0.0.0.9.f.0.0.e.f.a.c.8.b.d.0.1.0.0.2.ip6.arpa    name =
suckerpunch.movie.edu.
```

If you're feeling masochistic, you could specify all 34 labels of the domain name that corresponds to the IPv6 address, in which case you must explicitly change the query type to *ptr*:

```
% nslookup
> set type=ptr
> 3.d.0.0.0.0.0.0.0.0.0.0.0.0.0.0.9.f.0.0.e.f.a.c.8.b.d.0.1.0.0.2.ip6.arpa.
Server:         terminator.v6.movie.edu.
Address: 2001:db8:cafe:1::1#53

3.d.0.0.0.0.0.0.0.0.0.0.0.0.0.0.9.f.0.0.e.f.a.c.8.b.d.0.1.0.0.2.ip6.arpa    name =
suckerpunch.movie.edu.
```

Of course, you can also do this from the command line, like so:

```
% nslookup -type=aaaa suckerpunch.movie.edu.
```

and

```
% nslookup 2001:db8:cafe:f9::d3
```

dig

The chief difference between *nslookup* and *dig* is that *dig* has no interactive mode: you specify everything at the command line. And *dig* is smart enough—in most cases—to differentiate between domain names and record types, so you can specify those in whichever order you like. To query a name server other than the first one in *resolv .conf*, type an @ followed by its domain name or IP address. As I mentioned earlier, if you use a domain name that owns both AAAA and A records, recent versions of *dig* will use the IPv6 address, so:

```
% dig @terminator.movie.edu. soa movie.edu.
```

has the same effect as

```
% dig @2001:db8:cafe:1::1 soa movie.edu.
```

To look up a AAAA record, just specify *aaaa* on the command line:

```
% dig aaaa suckerpunch.movie.edu.
```

or

```
% dig suckerpunch.movie.edu. aaaa
```

Either way, the output will look something like this:

```
; <<>> DiG 9.8.0 <<>> suckerpunch.movie.edu. aaaa
;; global options: +cmd
;; Got answer:
;; ->>HEADER<<- opcode: QUERY, status: NOERROR, id: 21059
;; flags: qr aa rd ra; QUERY: 1, ANSWER: 1, AUTHORITY: 2, ADDITIONAL: 5

;; QUESTION SECTION:
;suckerpunch.movie.edu.          IN      AAAA

;; ANSWER SECTION:
suckerpunch.movie.edu.   86400   IN      AAAA    2001:db8:cafe:f9::d3

;; AUTHORITY SECTION:
movie.edu.         86400    IN    NS    terminator.movie.edu.
movie.edu.         86400    IN    NS    wormhole.movie.edu.

;; ADDITIONAL SECTION:
terminator.movie.edu.    86400   IN    A      192.249.249.1
terminator.movie.edu.    86400   IN    AAAA   2001:db8:cafe:1::1
wormhole.movie.edu.      86400   IN    A      192.249.249.3
wormhole.movie.edu.      86400   IN    A      192.253.253.3
wormhole.movie.edu.      86400   IN    AAAA   2001:db8:cafe:2::1

;; Query time: 3 msec
;; SERVER: 127.0.0.1#53(127.0.0.1)
;; WHEN: Sun Mar 27 19:42:46 2011
;; MSG SIZE  rcvd: 219
```

To reverse-map an IPv6 address, avail yourself of the handy -x command-line option, which takes an IPv6 address (rather than its equivalent 34-label domain name) as an argument:

```
% dig -x 2001:db8:cafe:f9::d3
```

One trick suggested by Owen DeLong, one of my technical reviewers, is to let *dig* do the hard work of creating the 34-label owner name of an IPv6 PTR record for you. For example, rather than laboriously typing the owner name that corresponds to 2620:0:930::400:933, you could simply run *dig -x 2620:0:930::400:933*:

```
% dig -x 2620:0:930::400:933

; <<>> DiG 9.6.0-APPLE-P2 <<>> -x 2620:0:930::400:933
;; global options: +cmd
;; Got answer:
;; ->>HEADER<<- opcode: QUERY, status: NXDOMAIN, id: 28788
;; flags: qr rd ra; QUERY: 1, ANSWER: 0, AUTHORITY: 1, ADDITIONAL: 0

;; QUESTION SECTION:
;3.3.9.0.0.0.4.0.0.0.0.0.0.0.0.0.0.0.0.0.0.0.3.9.0.0.0.0.0.0.2.6.2.ip6.arpa. IN PTR
...
```

Then copy the owner name from the line below `;; QUESTION SECTION` and paste it into your zone data file.

Like *nslookup*, *dig* digs the abbreviated form of the IPv6 address. If you want to do it the hard way, you'll have to specify the PTR query type on the command line:

```
% dig ptr 3.d.0.0.0.0.0.0.0.0.0.0.0.0.0.9.f.0.0.e.f.a.c.8.b.d.0.1.0.0.2.ip6.arpa.
```

Get even more for your money.

Join the O'Reilly Community, and register the O'Reilly books you own. It's free, and you'll get:

- $4.99 ebook upgrade offer
- 40% upgrade offer on O'Reilly print books
- Membership discounts on books and events
- Free lifetime updates to ebooks and videos
- Multiple ebook formats, DRM FREE
- Participation in the O'Reilly community
- Newsletters
- Account management
- 100% Satisfaction Guarantee

Signing up is easy:

1. **Go to: oreilly.com/go/register**
2. **Create an O'Reilly login.**
3. **Provide your address.**
4. **Register your books.**

Note: English-language books only

To order books online:

oreilly.com/store

For questions about products or an order:

orders@oreilly.com

To sign up to get topic-specific email announcements and/or news about upcoming books, conferences, special offers, and new technologies:

elists@oreilly.com

For technical questions about book content:

booktech@oreilly.com

To submit new book proposals to our editors:

proposals@oreilly.com

O'Reilly books are available in multiple DRM-free ebook formats. For more information:

oreilly.com/ebooks

Spreading the knowledge of innovators | oreilly.com

The information you need, when and where you need it.

With Safari Books Online, you can:

Access the contents of thousands of technology and business books

- Quickly search over 7000 books and certification guides
- Download whole books or chapters in PDF format, at no extra cost, to print or read on the go
- Copy and paste code
- Save up to 35% on O'Reilly print books
- **New!** Access mobile-friendly books directly from cell phones and mobile devices

Stay up-to-date on emerging topics before the books are published

- Get on-demand access to evolving manuscripts.
- Interact directly with authors of upcoming books

Explore thousands of hours of video on technology and design topics

- Learn from expert video tutorials
- Watch and replay recorded conference sessions

Spreading the knowledge of innovators   safari.oreilly.com

CPSIA information can be obtained at www.ICGtesting.com
Printed in the USA
265771BV00003B/38/P